Beautiful Birds

HUMMINGBIRDS

By Kristen Rajczak Nelson

Gareth Stevens
PUBLISHING

Please visit our website, www.garethstevens.com. For a free color catalog of all our high-quality books, call toll free 1-800-542-2595 or fax 1-877-542-2596.

Library of Congress Cataloging-in-Publication Data

Names: Rajczak Nelson, Kristen, author.
Title: Hummingbirds / Kristen Rajczak Nelson.
Description: New York : Gareth Stevens Publishing, [2023] | Series: Beautiful birds | Includes index.
Identifiers: LCCN 2021035975 (print) | LCCN 2021035976 (ebook) | ISBN 9781538275160 (set) | ISBN 9781538275177 (library binding) | ISBN 9781538275153 (paperback) | ISBN 9781538275184 (ebook)
Subjects: LCSH: Hummingbirds–Juvenile literature.
Classification: LCC QL696.A558 R35 2023 (print) | LCC QL696.A558 (ebook) | DDC 598.7/64–dc23
LC record available at https://lccn.loc.gov/2021035975
LC ebook record available at https://lccn.loc.gov/2021035976

First Edition

Published in 2023 by
Gareth Stevens Publishing
29 East 21st Street
New York, NY 10010

Editor: Kristen Nelson
Designer: Andrea Davison-Bartolotta

Photo credits: Cover Martin Pelanek/Shutterstock.com; p. 1 Brian A Wolf/Shutterstock.com; p. 5 Milan Zygmunt/Shutterstock.com; p. 7 James Bloor Griffiths/Shutterstock.com; p. 9 (left) Paul Wittet/Shutterstock.com; pp. 9 (bottom right), 11, 17, 24 (bill) Ondrej Prosicky/Shutterstock.com; p. 9 (top right) Martin Mecnarowski/Shutterstock.com; pp. 13, 24 (wings) Petr Simon/Shutterstock.com; p. 15 Richard Seeley/Shutterstock.com; p. 19 Brent Barnes/Shutterstock.com; pp. 21, 24 (eggs) Daniel Lamborn/Shutterstock.com; p. 23 Damsea/Shutterstock.com.

Printed in the United States of America

CPSIA compliance information: Batch #CSGS23: For further information contact Gareth Stevens, New York, New York at 1-800-542-2595.

Contents

Hummingbirds are birds.
There are more than
300 kinds.

They are all small.

They can be many colors.
They can be green!

They have a long bill.

Their wings move fast.
It sounds like a hum.

They can fly up
and down.
They can fly backward.

They drink nectar.
It is found in flowers.

Sometimes they eat bugs.

Their nests are tiny.
Their eggs are white.

Babies come out of eggs. They do not have feathers.

Words to Know

bill

eggs

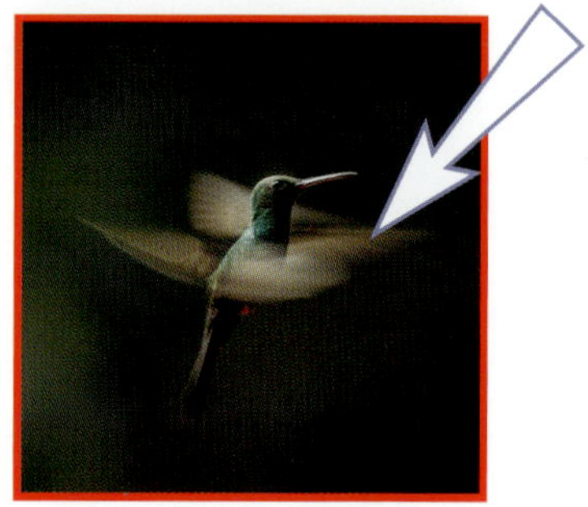

wings

Index